FINTO THE FOX

Written by Peter Aykroyd
Illustrated by Rhiannon Powell

Collins Educational

An imprint of HarperCollins*Publishers*

Finto crept silently but swiftly through the dark across the Common. His ears were pricked up and his nose twitched. He padded from bush to bush, from tree to tree, across ditches and paths. Every few steps he paused to listen, to smell. He was aware of distant traffic noises and, at times, of people calling and laughing. He didn't take much notice of these sounds, for he was on the lookout for his enemy.

Finto was a red dog fox. He had a reddish-brown coat which was white underneath and a bushy tail which was also white. His amber eyes were like a cat's, with slits which glowed in the dark when sudden light shone on them. His nose had a keen sense of smell, and his ears could hear a watch tick ten metres away. Finto was clever. He knew how to live, find food and survive in a populated town.

Finto lived in the wild part of the Common on the edge of the town, just as his ancestors had before him. Years ago, Finto's great grandfather had discovered the Common when he moved from the countryside into the town. The old fox had discovered it after trotting along railway cuttings and embankments. This wild patch was overgrown with brambles, bushes and weeds. Like all foxes, Finto had marked his patch with his scent to tell other foxes that it was his territory.

As Finto padded along this particular night, he sniffed for his enemy. This enemy was not the squirrels that lived in the plane trees where pigeons also perched, cooing. Nor the horses that were ridden along the paths, nor the cats and dogs that came from the houses built beside the Common. Finto just ignored cats as they watched him warily when he went by and he was not afraid of dogs. Or at least, not of most dogs. Just one of them was his enemy, Hassler.

Hassler was a dark-coated hunt terrier that prowled the Common by himself, day or night. He was a fierce fighter and he hated foxes. Finto always knew when Hassler was close because of the terrier's strong smell and loud snuffle. The fox always slipped away when he knew his enemy was near because he never forgot the time Hassler once surprised him in the daytime.

Finto had been asleep, lying under some old tree roots. He had sprinted away but the faster dog gained on him. Fortunately, Finto had reached a large patch of brambles just in time and had sped down a path in the thorny bushes which was too narrow for Hassler to follow. After that escape, Finto took even more care to avoid his enemy. He would cock his head to listen and sniff for the terrier when he sensed that dogs were close by, just as he was doing tonight.

Finto lived and hunted alone, like all dog foxes, but he brought food to his mate, Bron, in her earth. He had mated with Bron at Christmas time after meeting her when she was eating the remains of a turkey she had discovered outside a restaurant. Finto began courting her with short barks and before long, Bron was calling back to him with howls. The two foxes had then hunted together over the Common.

It had been within a few weeks of mating that Bron settled to have her litter. Bron had dug the den which became her earth under an old garden shed which backed on to the Common. She had not made a nest of any kind, but had given birth to her four cubs on the bare soil of the earth. That was in March. The cubs – two male, two female – were born with woolly, dark-brown fur and short rounded snouts.

After only four weeks, Tal, Tas, Teg and Tod had grown big enough to go outside to play.

Outside the earth lay an old log. Here the cubs had been playing together for the last two weeks, just like kittens. They had fought, chased each other, run up and down the log, and stalked anything that moved, from insects to leaves blown in the wind. Teg was the strongest and the boldest, jumping on twigs, old bones, and sometimes on his father when Finto came to visit his family.

Whenever Finto searched for food, watching out for Hassler, he knew Bron was taking care of their cubs. When danger was near from people or animals, Bron would give one short scream and chase her cubs into the earth. They would all wait there until it was safe to come out. Bron always had to grab Teg by the scruff of the neck and carry him into the earth because he always wanted to stay and see what the danger was.

Now that he was six weeks old and growing redder in colour, Teg had begun to explore the bushes beyond the log. Several times he had lost his way, but a yelp always brought Bron's answering bark to tell him where she was.

If Finto could have seen what was happening at home while he was hunting on this night, he would have returned to the earth at once. For Teg was in trouble. He had scampered away through the under-growth, going further than he had ever been.

Hearing the squeak of a mouse in a bramble bush, Teg crouched down and prepared to pounce on the little creature. The mouse kept still and quiet and Teg was so interested in his prey that he didn't hear Bron's warning bark. When he got bored with waiting, he dashed out of the bramble bush, nearly head on into Hassler!

Teg stopped short, quivering and rigid with shock. He tried to make himself run away, but he couldn't move at all. It was too late to escape. Hassler seized Teg in his slathering jaws and threw him into the air. The cub landed on his back, whimpering with pain. The dog pounced on him, growling, snuffling and showing his teeth. Teg smelled his tormentor's hot breath and waited for painful bites. Then Hassler paused. His ears pricked up. He had heard an anguished howling behind him.

Bron had arrived from the earth, even though she was afraid to leave the other cubs unattended. Bravely she stood behind the dog, snarling softly. Hassler whirled around, fur bristling. He had to let go of Teg so that he could bark with fury, giving Teg a chance to get away, especially if Hassler decided to fight Bron. But Teg's feet still wouldn't work.

Hassler moved slowly towards Bron, heaving with anger, ready to attack. Then sounds nearby made him stop. The sounds were the warning growls of Barkis and Hunter, two dogs that had followed him across the Common.

Barkis was a large, shaggy mongrel and Hunter was a tough beagle hound. When they scented the fox cub, the dogs barked and barked with excitement. They wanted the cub, too. Hassler couldn't beat both in a fight, so he picked Teg up again and ran off quickly with Barkis and Hunter in pursuit. Bron watched the three dogs disappear with her son in Hassler's jaws. She trotted after them for a short distance but soon stopped.

Hassler and Teg were too far away for her to follow and she couldn't leave her other three cubs.

Bron slipped back to her earth where Tod, Tal and Tas were shaking with fear. Bron could do nothing to rescue Teg now. She lay comforting her cubs and soon they fell asleep, tired out from play and the fright of the evening. Later, Bron would slip out of the earth for a short time to find some food for the next day.

14

Late that night, Finto returned to the earth. He picked up Hassler's scent mingled with Teg's and the two other dogs', and knew at once that Teg was in danger. He didn't stop. He touched noses with Bron and set off into the dark trailing Hassler by the mingling scents along the way.

Finto had to follow Hassler to the terrier's home in a

block of flats on the shady side of the Common. To get
there he had to go across the busy main road, then over
the open grass of the football pitches.

Darkness still covered the Common. The only lights
were the street lamps along the main road, a few lights
on the main paths and a few others overlooking the
wide, open ground. Finto loped on as fast as he could.

Meanwhile, what had happened to Teg? When
Hassler had grabbed him and run off, with Barkis and
Hunter following, Teg was held tightly in the terrier's
jaws. Hassler had kept off the paths so that he and Teg
were very difficult to see. At the main road, Hassler
had dashed across a gap in the traffic, gripping Teg
more tightly. Hunter and Barkis still tore after him.

Before long, Hassler came to the fences and hedges of
the row of houses which backed on to the Common.

He was nearly home. Suddenly, he stopped. He
pinned Teg down under his paws and snarled viciously
at his pursuers. At first, the two dogs drew back. They
then crept forward slowly, still barking, ready to tear his
prey away. The dogs crouched down to attack. Hassler
got to his feet, ready to fight them. Teg was free again,
but still he was too scared and weak to run away.

Just then, a boy and a girl ran out of the garden gate of one of the houses. The boy shone a torch to see what the barking was all about. At the sight of the three dogs, he and the girl acted quickly. They shooed the hound and the mongrel away easily, but Hassler stayed, barking loudly. By the light of the torch, the children could see the frightened fox club lying behind the terrier. The two ran at Hassler, shouting, and the boy waved the torch. Hassler was taken by surprise.

Snorting angrily, he fled into the dark.

19

The boy and the girl looked at Teg closely, and saw that he was unharmed apart from some bite marks and deep scratches. Teg was terrified by these two new and strange creatures with their unfamiliar smells. Would they hurt him, too? The girl picked Teg up and carried him to an empty rabbit hutch in their garden.

Inside the hutch was some straw, and outside a short run covered with wire-netting. Teg snapped at the girl in fright as she laid him gently on the straw. The boy fetched a saucer of warm milk and a plate of meat scraps from the house and placed them beside the cub.

The children then left him to rest. Teg was too afraid to touch the food. He lay in the straw, sad and cold. It was the first time he had ever spent the night away from the earth.

Before long, however, Teg heard the scary snuffling and growling of Hassler again. He saw the dog squeeze through a hole in the fence and run up to the hutch. He watched Hassler try to break through the wire-netting and then start to dig a hole under the wire. Teg whimpered and tried to shrink as far as he could into the back of the hutch. The hole grew deeper and deeper.

After a while, a loud whistle from the nearby block of flats stopped Hassler digging. He hesitated, then obeyed his owner's call. His owner took Hassler for a walk, safely attached to a lead. But the dog kept looking back to the garden and his prey.

Meanwhile, Finto was still following Hassler's scent which was very strong and easy for him to trail. Every now and then, Finto could also smell Teg where the cub's body had touched the branch of a bush or long blades of grass. At the main road, he dashed across, recklessly. He was lucky to get across unhurt.

Finally, Finto arrived at the houses overlooking the Common. He approached the area carefully. His nose told him what had taken place as clearly as if he had been there. He knew that the two other dogs and two humans had been there not long before. Teg had been placed on the ground. Hassler had moved off, but not with the cub. So Teg must be near. Finto barked once, softly. He cocked his head, so that his ears could hear sounds from all directions.

Then he heard it. A small cry. The call of a sad, lonely, little fox cub.

Finto ran towards Teg's voice. He slipped through the small gap in the hedge used by Hassler. In front of him was the hutch, and in it was a delighted cub. Teg limped to the side of the run. He tried to lick Finto through the wire-netting, but the holes were too small.

Finto knew he must free Teg quickly, before Hassler returned. He saw the hole the dog had started to dig, but didn't go on digging because he could see that the floor of the run was also made out of wire. He couldn't get Teg out that way, but Hassler could do Teg further harm through the netting.

The fox circled the hutch, pawing the wooden slats until he found one at the back which seemed loose. Finto grasped the end of the slat in his teeth, braced his legs and pulled. The nails holding the end of the slat gave way easily. Finto held the slat away from the hutch and Teg had just enough room to squeeze through. Slowly and painfully the little cub climbed out as Finto kept alert for any sound of Hassler, Barkis or Hunter.

Finto was very pleased to see his son and licked him once hurriedly, for they could not waste time. Finto moved towards the Common to start their long journey home. Teg was stiff and could only limp along slowly after him. Finto tried to hurry. He pushed Teg gently with his nose to make him go faster but although Teg was losing his stiffness, one leg still hurt badly. Every now and then, the pain made him squeal.

Father and son had just reached the silver birch trees on the Common when a sound not far away made their ears prick up with fear. It was the loud snuffle of a dog and it was coming closer, fast. Only one dog snuffled like that. Hassler. The dog's deep snuffle told Finto how close Hassler was behind them. More worried than ever, Finto again tried to make his little son move along more quickly. Teg complained with a small whine and sat down, feeling sore and tired. Finto knew that he would have to stop and fight his larger and stronger enemy. But he wanted to choose the place that would give him an advantage in the fight.

Finto and Teg were near a shallow ditch that twisted across the Common. Rain showers the afternoon before had filled the ditch with water and Finto acted quickly. He pushed Teg into the ditch and jumped in to pull the cub along for a few metres. Teg hated this but the cold shock of the water stopped him from crying out at first. Finto left the distressed cub in a muddy pool and jumped out of the ditch. Teg began to shiver and whimper with fear and weariness once more.

Finto's action confused Hassler as the water dulled the smell of the foxes. However, he kept creeping forward and came to the ditch. Hassler jumped into the ditch, nose twitching at the faint fox smells. Then he heard Teg's cries further along the ditch. Trailing the lead he still wore, Hassler splashed happily through the water towards the sound of the prey he was hunting. He was not listening out for any other noises.

Suddenly, silently, Finto attacked. He sprang down
into the ditch and seized Hassler's neck with his jaws.
The terrier was taken completely by surprise. He was
knocked off balance and fell over yelping with pain but
raked the claws of his powerful back legs against Finto's
underside. The fox had to let go quickly. Hassler,
howling with rage, rolled over on to his feet. He bit
painfully into Finto's shoulder.

Finto yowled and tore himself away, leaping out of
the ditch. Hassler followed him, snapping at his bushy
tail. The fox spun around and attacked the dog again,
biting his nose. The two fighters rolled over and over
together, biting, scratching, barking, growling, snarling.
The noise of the fight and the sound of Hassler
frightened Teg into running away. He staggered along
the ditch, found a low bank and climbed out. He
wanted to go home.

Out of the ditch, Teg didn't know where he was, but then he came across the tracks Hassler had made when he had come to the earth earlier. Using his nose like a grown-up fox, he made his way slowly towards home.

Behind him, he could hear the yelps and angry howls of the battle. The noise frightened him, but he kept on going. Suddenly, the sound of fighting stopped. Teg sat down. Who had won? He sniffed the silent air.

Teg waited, trembling, little ears tuned to catch every murmur of noise. Then he heard an animal creep slowly towards him. The cub crouched low in fright.

Then he raised his tail in delight. It was Finto, but a Finto in great pain. Like Teg, he was limping and he was covered in bite marks and scratches, most of which were bleeding. He also had a badly torn ear. Finto glanced behind him, then nuzzled his son. Teg rubbed himself along his father's coat. Now they would soon get home.

The fight had ended when the end of Hassler's lead had caught in a root and he couldn't pull himself free to continue the chase. Finto had not waited a moment more. He had set off, as fast as he could hobble, to find his son.

Now that he had found Teg, Finto nudged the cub to make him move as fast as possible, but neither he nor Teg could move very quickly. They both felt very sore and they had to stop and rest many times. Even the main road seemed a long way ahead of them.

The sky was getting light when they reached the road. Finto pushed Teg under a bench for another short rest.

Teg was glad to lie down but after only a few minutes, Finto made him get to his feet again. They could not waste any more time. The cub cried with tiredness. At the edge of the road, they paused again. There was not much traffic, but Finto waited for a moment when the road was clear. Then he shoved Teg on to the hard surface, growling to make his little son cross quickly.

Teg was bewildered by the lights. When they had nearly crossed the road, he stopped, held by the headlights of a car speeding towards them. Finto moved fast. He seized Teg by the scruff of the neck and dragged him, squealing, out of the way, the car missing them by a few centimetres. They rested again by the roadside, by a holly bush. Finto began to feel exhausted. His legs were becoming stiff from their wounds, but they had to keep moving as it would soon be day. Father and son again set off, painfully.

Then Finto stopped suddenly by a clump of birch trees. He had heard behind them the sound they feared most of all, the sound of a snuffling dog. Hassler was coming after them yet again! He had finally pulled his lead clear and was able to gain on the two tired foxes.

Finto shivered. He was in worse shape than Hassler and slowing up more and more. But he and Teg were near the end of their trek. The cub also sensed he was close to home. Pain forgotten, Teg bounded ahead.

Behind them, Hassler howled as the scent of the foxes got stronger. Teg reached the entrance of the earth first and saw his mother waiting for him. He wanted to snuggle her, but Bron quickly shoved him into the earth.

Finto plodded painfully up to his mate. They touched noses and he limped straight into her home.

Bron waited for Hassler, silent, eyes and ears alert. Soon, the terrier loped towards her, growling, snuffling. To his surprise, she barked and crouched down, ready to spring at him.

Hassler had expected to fight a wounded fox, not a fresh one. He stopped. He knew he could not win this fight for the cub. Bron crept forward, showing her teeth. Hassler drew back, turned and slunk away.

Bron watched Hassler until he was out of sight beyond the trees. Then she slipped into the earth. Earlier, she had found a large bone with meat on it in the rubbish bins behind her favourite restaurant. Now she chased the excited cubs away from the bone and took it over to Finto. Lying down, he began to gnaw it with pleasure.

Bron began to lick his wounds. Teg came close and Finto growled. Teg sat still until a grunt from Finto told him that he too, could have some meat and a lick of his sores.